GW01313698

THE YUMS

Garlic had very smelly feet

which made her terribly shy

She didn't know
what caused the whiff

She could think of
no reason why

'Perhaps I have stepped
into something yucky'

She was in a right to-do!

'It could have been
something very mucky

like a pile of doggy poo'

People who happened
to come along

would hold their nose
and say 'Cor!'

One little girl found
the pong so strong

that she fainted
onto the floor

Garlic tried putting
boots on her feet

to cover the awful stink

but the odour fantastic
burned through the plastic

It was truly much worse
than you think

Garlic sat in the fridge
to try to stay fresh

'The cold might make
me less niffy'

But the other food there
was filled with despair

and bundled her out in a jiffy

She was alone in the room
when along came
mushroom

who said
'I don't want
to upset you ...'

'But the smell that you think
only comes from your feet

comes from your
whole body too!'

'Please don't be sad
things aren't really that bad

Dad likes food
with a good whifferoo'

'There is nothing wrong
with a bit of a pong

and nothing whiffs
quite like you!'

The Yums

Created by Mary Ingram

Read about Garlic's friends ...

www.theyums.co.uk

Printed in Great Britain
by Amazon